M●RE PIE, *please*

USING GROWTH POLES TO REDUCE SUFFERING

David Thulin

ISBN: 9781543967081   ISBN eBook: 9781543967098

NOW

It should be everybody's dream to make the world a better place. A life lived only reacting is a life wasted. Taking charge and moving the world along should be the norm. Alas, it is not. Striving to end global suffering is even a rarity – we only care about our own back yard, about our immediate environment. Those of us in the Western world seem to be generally focused only on ensuring that we will not be personally inconvenienced. Yet, while you read this paragraph, a child somewhere died of starvation, a mother died in childbirth, and a previously healthy person died of a curable disease.

But there is hope. Things can be done. This is a story – not a dry academic text full of citations – about how the beginning of the end of global suffering could be achieved: we have almost all the technology, and we certainly have all the minds and all the funds. What is lacking? The will. Lack of will stems in part from lack of short-term financial profits and in part from unclear long-term gains. Empathy rarely changes this profit-driven behavior. What remains hidden to most is that ethically sound business – like today's shift towards renewable energy – is financially smart business. At least, given sufficient time. However, profit is not the only thing that motivates people to help others. Curiosity, empathy, and willingness to develop ideas also play a role. It is not often one sees how a single disruptor can lead to massive changes practically overnight – changes that spread much wider than is immediately obvious. For instance, the same research behind electric cars leads to longer-lasting flashlights and batteries for off-grid electricity networks and new highly efficient solar cells make truly wireless security cameras and other wireless electronics readily available.

This ability for change to spread and affect adjacent industries is an example of the first mechanism that can help save humanity. Such spreading of development is practically inevitable, and it is true geographically as well. This idea is generally referred to as the "growth pole" phenomenon – a theory developed in the 1950s by Francois Perroux. It says, very basically, that development doesn't occur equally everywhere at once. Future development usually takes place close to previous development. This has been shown over and over again. For example, a modern subway system was built in Ethiopia and shortly afterwards, Ethiopian Airlines was one of the first customers for Boeing's new Dreamliner. Cause and effect? Causality might be difficult to prove, but fully unrelated they are not.

The second mechanism is significantly more difficult, but not exactly for the reason you might think. We must empower the whole population, primarily women. There are strong forces opposing this. Primitive thought, stemming mostly from religion, finds it somehow threatening to stop treating women as second-class citizens. Women without hope seem to fit perfectly into many religiously based societies. However, when women aren't empowered in a society, that society is effectively using only half of its resources (in this case, people), which does not seem to be a winning concept.

The core idea presented within this book is to select a suitable region, fabricate a growth pole quickly, and simultaneously empower women. Through these mechanisms, along with smart planning and even smarter execution, the selected region will quite likely see drastic, even life-altering, improvements. Some of these changes will be immediate, while some will start slow but grow immense with time!

I realize that some parts of my plan are naive, and I do assume a lot. On the other hand, much of this can be done today, and some effects are better than none. A mobile water purification plant and some diesel fuel deployed today could save lives! (That is a literal statement. With a machine that already exists and readily available fuel, people currently dying of thirst or giving birth without clean water will survive. Today. Now.) In fact, money enough for hundreds of such water purification systems is already being spent on things like a trip to Mars and devastating wars in developing countries. Opening a commercial route to Mars is noble and may in the end be necessary for the survival of our species – but spending billions on inter-planetary travel is a bit hard to swallow when several million children under five die yearly of diseases for which we found the cure ages ago and of imminently solvable problems like starvation and thirst.

One of the major challenges facing this plan, as with most efforts to change the status quo, will be the potential for violence wherever we decide to try it. Many of Earth's poorest regions are also the most war-torn. In many areas, the only technically sophis-ticated machines that are widely available are designed to kill human beings. As I see it, this can be tackled in one of two very different ways: we can "rent" the French Foreign Legion and make certain they always fire first, saving humanity with fear, as it were. Or, infinitely more likely, we can enter the area chosen for this experi-ment completely unarmed. We would begin by speaking to tribal elders, locals, and even leaders of opposing military factions. We would explain in detail exactly what will be done, and where, and hear and incorporate their opinions. Local inclusion in all planning is critical. Then, perhaps we begin with a low-risk "campaign of kind-ness" through which we "soften up" the population with some weeks of daily air drops of food and water and basic hygiene equipment like soap and toothbrushes. Shock and awe, but in reverse.

A second major challenge is the different ways people experience and expect fairness. First, we cannot claim that this or any plan is universally fair according to everybody, at all times, equally. Such fairness is literally impossible. There are hundreds of places that desperately need help. Saving a child *here* in essence means not saving a child *there*. A good friend of mine tells his children now and then that life simply is not fair. And the older I get and the more I see, the more I realize that something is wrong with this world and that my friend is spot-on correct. So, this plan will immediately help a small region of the world. Are other regions perhaps more deserving? Sure. Have we actively decided NOT to help region X? Nope. Can I guarantee this will work? Again, no. But if it does, a part of the world will be better, and we can do it again, and if it does not work, a part of a country will be better and we will have gained important experience on which to base our next effort.

It must be noted that certain countries are cynically making investments in the third world in exchange for global political influence in the United Nations (UN) central assembly. These are some of the richest countries in the developed world, some of those countries that would gain the most from a successful developing world. This is done in a way that is terrifyingly familiar: colonialism. Such exploitation cannot be allowed to proceed. We must see the developing world as more than a source of cheap labor and natural resources.

THE CURE FOR POVERTY

First, let's talk about what real poverty is and is not:

It is not having to choose between movies or eating out. It is not about living in subsidized housing. For the purposes of this book, it means having to choose which of your children will survive. It means dealing with life and death daily.

The cure for poverty is no secret. It has been known for years. Maybe not a cure *per se*, but a way to end it. The cure even has a name: the empowerment of women. Give women control of their reproductive cycle, give them credit and a bag of seeds, and watch the collective floor of their society slowly but surely rise.

The rising happens far beyond the area where women are being empowered. Good things have an odd way of spreading. Female-led development is contagious. Unfortunately, this approach faces powerful resistance. Not only is religion hell bent on treating women as only good for reproduction (the catholic notion that "condoms are worse than AIDS" surely doesn't help either), but there is also a tendency among developed nations to use and abuse poorer nations, particularly those in Africa, for natural resources. The amounts of such resources that are available are nothing short of mind boggling: from millions of tons of precious minerals and stones to fine woods, resources are snatched up in what any civilized person would consider highway robbery, not to mention the lack of regard for the short- and long-term effects on the environment. Regardless of the resistance this plan will face, the goal of this project must be to raise the floor for all humanity.

Another rarely discussed problem is the negative effect of charity given with good intentions. First-world citizens often try to "buy a conscience" by giving money to various charities. These donations are almost always certainly well intended, yet they almost without fail lead to increased corruption and well-lined pockets for a very few.

Finally, everything must be sped up. The kind of growth pole we want to develop does not have the luxury of several generations of time – yet the process can't be too fast. A perfect example of the mess that can result from too much change too fast is Uganda: after Idi Amin expelled all Asians over the course of just a few weeks, he basically dropped full businesses and factories into the laps of an untrained and unmotivated local population. As you might expect, chaos ensued, and the Ugandan economy crashed. Apart from his actions being incredibly racist and dumb, change simply does not work like that. Giving people the keys to the car doesn't mean they know how to drive. Instead, we need to provide people with many easy opportunities they are ready and able to take advantage of to improve their lives.

A CITY UNITED

How do we measure national development? A plethora of variables spring to mind: childhood mortality, literacy and education, poverty rates... Whatever we choose to guide us, there will be omissions, and there will be great arguments to include the variables that are not chosen. One of the better indicators looks at where people live and what kinds of communities they live in. For anything to happen, people need to meet. At a very basic level, development and progress of any kind demands human interaction. If we remain solitary, our ideas will go nowhere at amazing speed – knowledge needs to be disseminated to be useful for more than one person.

This is part of why the richest places on earth tend to be urban, or at least densely populated. Look no further than Hong Kong or Singapore. Vice versa, the poorest areas tend to be very spread out – look at Mali or Burundi. The better off people are, the more eager they seem to be to live a city life. The correlation is not perfect, but it generally holds true. One major part of the explanation is this: when you are very poor, there is no advantage to centralized living. At the very beginning of human development, people are subsistence farmers, so they need space. It has been calculated that even with modern small farming techniques, one person needs one acre to survive – imagine the space needed for a family of ten equipped with only the most primitive tools. People are farming to survive. In some places, almost everyone farms! One person must farm his or her own food and each parent must farm enough to feed themselves and their children. As technology is introduced, a shift occurs: suddenly, a single person farming can feed ten people! And this number keeps increasing – into the thousands in some places – and that results in more and more people being free to do something *besides* farming.

These people start doing new things, like manufacturing or creating art, and begin to see the advantages of living in close proximity to others, which allows them to sell their products or exhibit their creations. Soon, companies form – because the entrepreneurial spirit always exists in some people – and companies want (and need) to be near sufficient sources of both labor and customers. Then people, in turn, want to be near the companies that are hiring, creating a positive feedback loop. So, wherever we decide to implement our growth pole plan, we can quite safely presume that the ideal place will have less than 50% of its national population already living in cities. We can also hope that this percentage will increase at a speed that is rapid enough to support virtuous cycles but not faster than infrastructure can handle. As we start doing things, we will be creating a demand – both temporary and permanent – for labor and services in the cities, so we don't really need to focus on this transfer of people specifically. If we do well, it will happen by itself.

However, we do need to ensure that those moving to cities are welcomed properly, especially in terms of sufficient infrastructure. I have seen companies pre-cast prison cells with prepared plumbing and electrical ready to be glued together like big Lego blocks. If we can find the money and methods to treat our fellow humans as caged animals, then I am confident we can find the money and methods to give our fellow humans a roof above their head. Pre-casting mini-apartments that could be easily shipped and set up is not only possible but practical.

POLES FOR GROWTH

Let's talk about the underlying core idea of growth poles. Originally, the theory of growth poles simply stated that development doesn't occur in equal amounts everywhere. Geographical clusters develop, and these clusters are referred to as poles. It is a theory only in the same way gravity is a theory; the proof is likely right outside your window. It might be a pole of ants (an ant hill) or a pole of people (a city) – whatever it may be, the existence of growth poles is quite undisputed and uncontroversial and obvious.

However, aid today is generally provided in a way quite opposite to this "law" of nature. Nations ask, intending well, "Who has it worst right now?" And who can blame them? Immediate short-term minimization of human suffering is a grand goal. This kind of aid distribution has been done for a long time, and while some progress has been made, our brothers and sisters are still starving to death.

Instead, I propose this: the introduction of an artificial growth pole with an unnaturally large – comparatively – development differential, introduced very quickly. Basically, introduce a few hundred years' worth of development to an area in only a few years and see how the surroundings react – like evolution on fast-forward. This evolution can – or rather, *should* – take some short cuts. Many parts of the traditional industrialization process can simply be skipped. (The world would hardly be a better place if ten thousand coal-burning factories suddenly appeared.) There are also some political experiments we need not and should not try again. Most serious analysis of politics agrees that democracy has flaws, but it sure beats everything else we have tested. For this artificial pole to be worthwhile, it must quite drastically reduce total suffering, both human and environmental, and it must generally improve every-thing. What is amazing is this: when we increase the developing world's slice of the pie, we are not reducing our own; we are making the pie bigger.

Still, there will be a romanticized "things were better before" movement or a "leave them alone" movement. The arguments are easy to make, albeit populistic, sloppy, and wrong. If you are scared by images of widespread consumerism and a million new fast food restaurants, then it is easy to see why this thought would exist. And to be honest, some things *were* better before, and some things in the Western world *should* be contained there. But a lot more was worse, and in some places has not improved. Like medicine. Or education. Or the fundamental individual belief that life is good and hopeful and that people should be free, independent of things like age or race.

In addition, there is an economic argument – a quite selfish one – for helping those in need. Developing nations donate hundreds of millions of dollars yearly to charity. But this money is far from enough (and/or possibly spent the wrong way, eventually lining the pockets of the corrupt): quadruple this amount and children will still starve to death *somewhere*. The plan presented here makes no claim to ending world hunger: I simply want to show a method that will probably help a larger area than, say, just air-dropping bottled water. I want to show a method that works and is repeatable. And that makes helping a smart thing to do.

So, what about this economic argument? Who should finance such a high-risk project? Well, everybody. We can all gain personally by ensuring that developing nations are better off. There is a strong argument for egoistic altruism. Everyone in the Western world will be better off – *individually* – when a billion new people become customers for (and crucially, are able to afford) cheap energy, better education, and smart healthcare. Somehow, with increased demand, we almost always see increased supply and lower costs.

Overwhelming a country with positivity is tricky, even if our intentions are good. Being nice on a global scale has been tried before – although sloppily and with many challenges that we need to avoid. Often we see well-intentioned donations of time or money go awry. It should be remembered that this growth pole does not intend to disseminate any specific political or religious views; we are simply trying to make sure that more people live a life free of unnecessary suffering.

DOLLARS AND SENSE

Everything that we do as part of this project must be transparent. What happens must be visible to all, and everyone should have the ability to get involved. People should care. Since we in the West, the wealthy few, don't appear to care much right now, something needs to change in the way we receive feedback after making a contribution of any sort. I think that the feedback must be immediate (or almost so) and the transparency must be total if we are to raise the funds and public interest needed to undertake this project.

Communication matters. Major organizations brag about the low proportion of donations that go to overhead costs. In Sweden, to be officially recognized as a nonprofit, the number must be lower than 10%. A key part of this plan is to keep administrative costs at a minimum, preferably far below 10%. This is probably vital to the success of the attempt to generate donations. To be able to say "you saved a life – no pockets were lined" is very powerful indeed.

Central to such transparency is a website filled with current information that is continually updated with images, movies, and text. This will demand full-time attention by one person practically from day one. Naturally, it will use modern techniques like virtual reality and 360° photos, but it can also use tested techniques like lots of live streams and minute-by-minute text updates. Weekly five-minute videos of updates and progress reports should be well produced and readily available. People tend to like consuming high-quality content. But our website must do more. Simply asking visitors to send money and giving a "thanks" in return will not do. First, what the project needs even more than money is skilled manpower. (Skilled is used lightly here – really, we should say motivated.) If volunteers want to live in a locally owned hotel and eat at a locally owned restaurant, then any skill they have is valuable because they are contributing doubly to the local economy. This might even start some "charitable tourism," through which even more money is injected into the local economy through spending at locally owned businesses. There could also be a micro-loan function focused exclusively on the selected area. We must show that small amounts can go a long way.

Micro-loans basically work like this: a person or a group asks for a smallish sum and presents a very brief business plan. These loans are then crowdfunded via a website that presents many such loan requests. (This would need to be managed by a separate company; many already exist.) One could perhaps think of this as a high-risk, low-reward activity. But most of these loans are repaid in full and on time. That being said, this is not something you do to make money; it is generally done out of the goodness of people's hearts and for the excitement of following the development of a business that you partly funded. The types of micro-loans that would benefit our growth pole would go toward things like buying livestock or a second taxi or building rooms for hire – giving birth to small businesses and helping them grow.

We, as humans, have an innate urge to help others. When faced with statements like "the money spent on your last coffee would have saved a child's life," we feel uneasy and we wish we could help or change something. Maybe it is only to calm our conscience, but the fact remains: we want to help. And one thing about our consumption-crazed society that is good for developing nations is that we all have stuff we don't need. Stuff can be useful, either put to its intended use or by being sold to raise funds. It all has to do with convenience. It must be easy to help – and it must be exciting! And feedback following donations must be on point and it must be quick. People who donate a box of crayons need to see the smiles of children coloring. Those who send mosquito nets need to see children alive. Coupling 'who-bought-what' with 'who-uses-what-when' may seem like an insurmountable challenge, but in reality, it is just a pain. And the world has lots of logistics experts who probably already have a solution. We have already started seeing climate compensation as a natural add-on to flights booked online – why not add some pencils or books to an online purchase? We could also raise money at supermarkets by connecting a big red button to the register. Press to round up! When it is absurdly easy to help, we are very generous. Especially if the people around us see how "good" we are.

POWERING UP

The question of energy is absolutely central to this work. This is so for several reasons, but primarily it's because we need a lot of it. Absolutely massive amounts. Enough, in fact, to open the door to any potential source of electricity. But the vetting is tough. We need to consider things such as cost, ease of expansion, and local physical impact. We also need to consider the environment: global warming is without any doubt already leading to unimaginable costs, and that trend is likely to continue. It is tempting to consider nuclear power: one modern plant can quite effortlessly power most any developing nation. But really, the argument for nuclear power that it is safe because an accident is highly unlikely is not a good one. "I'll walk around with this bomb – there's almost no chance it will explode." The very idea sounds silly. Besides, a nuclear power plant is extremely expensive, takes years to build, makes you dependent on mining or expensive imports, causes environmental disasters, and is limited in its expansion at best.

How about oil or gas? Perhaps even sourced locally? There are myriad reasons why this is simply foolish. First, it is a short-term solution: oil and gas *will* run out. Second, the infrastructure needed is immense: no country needs dangerous oil and gas pipelines or trucks fully laden with explosives zipping back and forth.

Even without considering carbon dioxide and harmful fumes and devastating spills or leaks, renewable energy – solar energy in particular – is the way to go. The one major drawback of solar we see in the West is the need for space. This may be a problem in Manhattan, but not so in many parts of the developing world. The math is easy. A couple of hundred acres of solar panels with good sun exposure can create more than enough power. The beauty is partly in the ease of expansion and partly in the minimal environmental impact. When and where space is practically unlimited, solar really shines. In fact, it has been calculated that with enough panels in the Sahara Desert, the whole planet's energy needs could be more than satisfied. Imagine the disruption of the world economy if Niger built a thousand-acre solar farm, making Africa energy independent. It would be beautiful.

But there are other potential sources of energy. Even in a slowly moving river, the energy-harvesting potential is decidedly massive. There are a few good ways to capture some of this energy. One method diverts a very small part of the river along a concrete channel and then sends it down into a vortex to spin a generator. Described somewhat clumsily, it works like this: Imagine a river with a 2° slope. Now divert a small portion of the flow to a cement-lined channel with a 1° slope. After some tens of meters, that water is well above the main river. Now, using a simple cement structure, make that water start moving in circles and drop it through a turbine down to river level, returning it to the river while powering the turbine. Another method involves the placement of large propeller blades or turbines directly in the river, which when turned by the river's flow generate electricity.

The main challenge with the first method is casting something with a consistent slope. However, this can be done centrally, and hydropower plants could be distributed with an all-wheel-drive truck and some laborers with a level and some shovels. A trained and well-supplied team of six could easily deploy four hydropower plants like this per week after a few months' worth of practice – out of the gate we can expect maybe half a plant a week. The second method demands much more skill, knowledge, and supervision. Maybe later.

There are several other options. Wood burning generators use a renewable source, but few things in the history of the world so perfectly combine massive maintenance requirements, complex design, and unreliability as do steam engines. Wood burning is a good source of heat and warm water. If the selected location needs either of those two things, wood burning will be revisited. The other clear option is wind power. Renewable, yes. But complicated, at least if the turbine is of any consequential size. And the complications grow exponentially if the turbine is at sea – energy harvesting potential is vastly increased, but so is difficulty of installation and maintenance. The notion that a wind turbine "just works" reflects reality poorly.

Around the world, our sources of energy must, and soon will be, solely renewable. Fighting this change is futile and potentially lethal. We mustn't allow our project to rely on the power generation methods of yesteryear.

LOCATION, LOCATION, LOCATION

The choice of location for the pole is very important. Like a farmer with their soil, we must ensure that conditions for growth are optimal. And it must be in the back of our collective mind that making a choice that is somehow wrong is possible, maybe even likely – but after all, only what we know *now* can influence the decisions we make *now*. Or, put another way: we can do everything right and still fail. That isn't necessarily failure, that's just life.

Political will is probably the single most important ingredient for success. One might think democracy and low levels of corruption are prerequisites. Alas, they aren't. Or rather, they are, but only *-ish*. (If childbirth is a potential death sentence, then fair elections are probably not your top priority.) Such requirements would simply disqualify too many possible locations. Democracy and low levels of corruption (often) go hand in hand and are a natural result of development – they are not mandatory for development in the first place. The natural evolution of a country from dictatorship to open democracy is a part of the growth we are trying to encourage. This might scare most dictators, but some of them might actually and honestly want the best for "their" country. Also, the area between democracy and dictatorship (or theocracy) is riddled with any number of government types. The grey zone is massive and a veritable minefield – we are looking for a country that is at least trying to move towards democracy.

Also, the choice cannot be based simply on how nice a people are. Interestingly, the less a people have, the more welcoming and generous they often are. Take Haiti, for example. Few countries, if any, have been dealt a worse hand, especially in recent years. They have tolerated cruel dictators, massive natural disasters, and endless – at times, almost calculatingly evil – exploitation of natural resources by the developed world, yet Haitians are some of the kindest and most positive people, in possession of an enviable drive and spirit. Yet for this project, Haiti is wrong: leaving the country or bringing materials into the country requires significant effort, for example sizable boats or air transport and the island is relatively close to powerhouse countries. As a result, the pole would be unlikely to find fertile soil for rapid development as defined by Francois Perroux.

A compelling argument can be made about India. We could not, perhaps, force development of the entire nation – it is simply too big – but we could work with a specific city. They are blessed with a pretty strong rail network (comparatively) and have a massive source of many problems: people still use the street as a toilet. If we somehow made public defecation a thing of the past, India would make significant gains in terms of health and development. However, India presents a few considerable challenges. First, of course, is the caste system. It is officially gone, but in reality, it is very much still there. Second is the belief embodied by Mother Theresa that human suffering is somehow a divine blessing. The ill, injured, and dying need a modern sterile hospital with well-educated, empathetic staff, not prayer. Also, India is already doing much of what I propose herein – although at a significantly slower pace – with good results.

The best bet is probably to start somewhere in Africa. The continent, its possibilities, and its problems are all huge. One of the challenges is HIV: in the Western world, that disease is no longer particularly dramatic – it's a big inconvenience, but one you will survive. That is not the case in many parts of Africa. This is partially due to distrust toward Western medicine in general, but mostly it is due to patent-holding medical companies that are more interested in their stock value than in human life. They really must learn that *ethically sound business always becomes financially sound business.* Being "good" seems to be the best form of marketing. The obvious place to look first is Botswana. Here is a country moving quickly in the "right" direction. If you take a look at any chart ranking African nations on almost anything, Botswana will be close to the top. Botswana's capital of Gabarone is a city that anyone with even the slightest interest in human development and potential really should visit. This is also, somewhat paradoxically, chief among the reasons why Botswana cannot be our target area: it is a country doing *too well.* I don't at all mean that Botswana is as well off as Denmark or France; I mean they are solidly on their way. And ten years from now, if nothing drastic goes wrong, Botswana will be significantly better off than it is today. In fact, we can already see a growth pole developing naturally: the neighboring countries of Zambia, Mozambique, and Namibia are all also increasing in freedom and general well-being.

While much of the low-hanging fruit has already been picked in Botswana, and the solid cultural opposition to helping those worst off is unlikely to change any time soon in India, the same can absolutely not be said about the former French colony the Central African Republic. In fact, the CAR – often called the "world champion of peacekeeping" – is a country filled to the brim with challenges and, to a Westerner, almost laughable omissions from the list of basic national needs. Additionally, cultural opposition in the CAR to equality of women is not as strong as it unfortunately still is in some countries. Some of these challenges are clear opportunities for a project such as this – the lack of a railway, for example. Or the absurdly high infant mortality rate. However, choosing a country with so many easily solved problems comes with major drawbacks. Major, as in civil war. Major, as in religiously and culturally motivated internal violence. Major, as in truly insane levels of corruption. But the low-hanging fruit, such as untapped resources, lots of rivers, and barely noticeable domestic energy consumption, is just so tempting.

When one hears "primitive town in Africa" or "refugee camp," an image might appear of leaky huts and a life of misery. But that is not always the actual case. Although the capital city of Bangui is in many ways considered the "worst" capital in the world, it is still a city with hotels, restaurants, and a hospital. However, many hundreds of thousands live in absolute poverty, without ready access to clean water and nutritious food. Many of the inhabitants are – generally speaking – desperate, and the gap between rich and poor is terrifyingly large. It is also at the core of many large and small conflicts, maybe not due to the gap size alone, but because those on the wrong side of the gap are quite literally dying.

However, when it comes down to it, there is one reason hovering above all others: Why not? The CAR deserves a break – the capital of Bangui is a friendly place and a great place to start. Few places deal on a daily basis with such enormous amounts of unnecessary suffering. The same argument could be used to motivate many choices, but you would be hard pressed to find a country with greater needs than the Central African Republic. Good results demand great preparation, so let's get started.

KNOWLEDGE IS POWER

First, we need to address the nature of this type of knowledge transfer. Or rather, we need to decide how many layers of knowledge we need to transfer. Put plainly, one person might be able to put the parts of a computer together, but that person doesn't know how to mine the copper, aluminum, and silicon or fabricate the necessary parts. In this case for example, Bangui needs plumbing but we don't need to learn how to make pipes. But thankfully, many of these steps can be skipped (as we have skipped them in the West) and simply outsourced – Bangui, the capital of CAR, does, after all, have an international airport with heavy machinery and computers, so we are not starting from the Stone Age.

That being said, especially with such lofty goals, we must start with simple and relatively small tasks. Like providing Bangui with clean water, nutrition, and a hygienic hospital. Gathering tens of tons of water will not be difficult. If push comes to shove, we can simply drive in ten tanker trucks per day filled with potable water from Europe – even when considering things like the risk of piracy and the cost of fuel, the costs are significantly lower than some of the more technical methods of getting "water from air" that you might read about in the press. These are frequently just glorified dehumidifiers, and they consume staggering amounts of energy. In countries where water is plentiful, it is painfully cheap for such a valuable commodity. In addition to taking water for granted, we need to realize that the cleanliness we take for granted in Western urgent care facilities (with hygiene a focus on everything, always, everywhere) is partially – but significantly – responsible for much of the medical success enjoyed in such facilities. So, getting some cleaning professionals with professional-level supplies to the Bangui hospital – both to do and to teach – is significant. We could recruit a well-oiled team from a Western (preferably French-speaking) hospital – to act like mercenaries of cleanliness.

We can start without lots of bureaucracy. Pretty much just call the local UN head and file a flight plan for the first inbound loads of water and food. Chat with the mayor of Bangui and the person in charge of the hospital, too. Being on good terms with the UN is a big deal. Some developing nations with ultra-high UN involvement are considered "UN countries;" the CAR is one of these, and the airport in Bangui is essentially UN-managed. When boarding the scheduled Air France Airbus A330 bound for Paris, your bags have, in fact, been screened by the United Nations – the same UN that mans the air traffic control tower which will guide your plane north.

While we overeat and overdrink in the West, people in less fortunate areas, like the CAR, are quite literally dying of starvation. Ending suffering from thirst and hunger must be our first goal. We will import the necessary items and collect them at gathering points within Bangui, like the hospital or gas stations. These distribution centers will be manned primarily by Bangui residents, although during the very first few weeks, they will likely be staffed by trainers and smiling international volunteers being trained to train. After all, this is a time when we are building much needed goodwill for the project, so smiles are needed. The stated goal here will be crystal clear: there will be NO suffering caused by thirst or hunger in Bangui. Within a few short months, the number of deaths caused by malnutrition will reach zero. To ensure everyone who needs help gets help, those manning these stations will be called upon to deliver items to the elderly, sick, and those otherwise unable to come to distribution points. The stations will be stocked and manned around the clock.

This phase must of necessity last a while. Much of what is coming depends on willing cooperation from locals and the blessing and support of those in charge. As they say: First impressions matter. Even when saving lives.

POLITICS OF FEAR

After a few months of consistent helping, our invading army of goodness will be considered with slightly less suspicion: time to supercharge our efforts. But this is not as simple as one might hope. Obstacles need to be circumvented and papers need to be signed. First, of course, we need to get the thumbs up from those in charge. Well, those *officially* in charge. The CAR has embassies in both Washington, DC, and Paris, but the people of CAR have much more in common with the French (so much so, in fact, that the first few dozen volunteers will probably need to all know at least *some* French) than with Americans, so to Paris we must go. Maybe even accompanied by the UN. (They get a lot of bad press due to childish and at times spectacularly stupid behavior by super powers in the Security Council, but the fact is that the UN directly saves lives each year.) This first meeting is absolutely tectonic in its importance. We should probably bring along either a well-known philanthropist or proof of some money being invested, as well as a CAR celebrity. Getting a "sure – go ahead and try," along with an "if it works, I get all the credit," will, with a smile from chance, make for smooth sailing. This will be the (comparatively) easy part.

Then comes the challenge at perhaps the very core of this entire plan. In Western media, the de facto rulers of the CAR are often referred to as "warlords." If that were true – or even somewhat accurate – things would actually be significantly easier. But these "warlords" are for the most part nothing but common thugs. With AK-47s. Thugs with AK-47s who are often illiterate and almost always uneducated. It is even rumored that Joseph Kony – a war criminal of epic proportions – is hiding in the CAR. He and others tend to use drugged-up and brainwashed juveniles as the core of their fighting force, since children tend to ask questions only after emptying a magazine or two. At least when they are high, drunk, disillusioned, and wholly without hope. This presents several sub-challenges. Getting cooperation and gaining trust from these "warlords" will demand a plethora of eclectic methods. One of them maybe wants a trip to an amusement park in Orlando, another wants his children in a school in Geneva. Those are both relatively easy requests to satisfy. And also: it does not have to work fully, everywhere, at once. It is not absolutely crucial that the whole country be weapons-free from day one. Eventually, of course, it will be necessary, but initially, some of these geniuses might find machine guns more attractive than mosquito repellent.

This pacification will be difficult outside of the capital city of Bangui. (The word "pacification" leaves a bad taste, courtesy of the Vietnam War. But we aren't trying to win an armed conflict in South East Asia in the early 1970s – we are trying to save lives here and now.) The first goal will be to rid the country of most firearms (being extra cautious about what groups remain armed) – we will initiate a cash/food/healthcare/travel/schooling-for-weapons pro-gram. (I am quite certain some Americans think weapons and an armed populous are powers for good. Some Americans are wrong.) Also, we must not forget: Bangui is a city of three quarters of a million people already living in *relative* safety. The risk of a random mad-man randomly killing people with an automatic weapon is quite small. As we widen our geographic sphere of influence (the areas where people are as safe from armed assaults as we are statistically in the West) to include rural communities, the capital will be at the center. We will center our pole on existing development. We will lead this expansion by air-dropping very basic items. Making sure that a few tons of water and food are dropped daily will not create enemies (hopefully). When it is deemed safe, we will visit these towns (collections of huts, really) with doctors, civil engineers, and local influencers.

There is really no schedule here: we can focus solely on ensuring that an area has plenty of food and water without doing anything else for months on end. Eventually, tribal elders and faction leaders will need to be addressed. It should be noted that we don't, won't, and shouldn't claim to be solvers of all problems – some quarrels might be several generations old. And these quarrels will likely make it impossible for everyone to meet under one roof at first. However, the main point now is to make one thing perfectly clear: we will never, under any circumstances, try to seize political power. And we will not impose our efforts without listening to the local population – their priorities might very well be different than ours. Countries in Africa have been promised so much and given so little. When we meet with local leaders, we will offer jobs and education and explain exactly what will be done, how it will be done, and when. But in the name of inclusion, we need to go further – every other week or so, we will meet again to report on progress and bring things like computers, TVs, VR helmets, and radio-controlled camera-equipped drones so that everyone can feel involved and up to date and so that citizens can experience first-hand the growth and development of their country.

One of the major powers we will be using to our advantage is a free, independent press and the freedom of speech. It is important to ensure that more than one outlet exists: with the natural curiosity of journalists and editors working in our favor and the speed of schools turning out newly trained and well-motivated youth (in the West and eventually in the CAR), staffing three or four weekly papers with international and local talent will not be a problem for long. We should also introduce radio channels. It is wise to ensure that from the start, the news outlets represent different opinions: maybe one conservative and one liberal. When the citizens feel free enough to criticize aspects of the project or to criticize the project as a whole, we will know we are succeeding.

BASIC NEEDS

With the leadership – both the official and actual – of the CAR at least semi-aboard, it has begun. Now for some dramatic development. It must begin in Bangui. The city will represent two growth poles at once – one within the CAR, centered in Bangui, and one in Northern Africa, centered in the CAR.

The contrasts within the CAR are truly terrifying. Bangui is a city with desperate needs. It is lacking in almost every way imaginable. But still, there is that direct flight to Paris. This flight, and indeed all others to Bangui, uses the Bangui airport, which is named M'Poko. It is no Western airport, but still, it has a relatively long paved runway. And land. Lots of land. Land that was and partially still is used as a makeshift refugee camp for the thousands of Central Africans who have been internally displaced by civil war.

The Bangui airport is laid out in a fairly traditional manner: one runway, all the buildings on one side, and two cement ramps (one civilian, one military/UN) and a dirt ramp for private aviation. No jetways. No centralized fuel system. There are huge overrun areas and there is not a single building on the west side of the runway – there is lots of room for expansion! The space and the location – in the middle of the city, like San Diego International or Dallas Love Field – are absolutely perfect for us in terms of being able, for instance, to quickly distribute arriving goods. With some luck and an alert customs workflow, water can quench thirst at the Bangui hospital an hour after it enters the country.

The first step will be to establish a non-threatening presence at M'Poko. We need a modern paved ramp, a warehouse, and offices. Volunteers will sleep at locally owned hotels, and all meals will be bought from local restaurants. After all, the whole purpose of this project is to inject massive positive movement into CAR's society and economy. Patronizing local companies is natural. (Vitally, people will be asked to eat locally but not told where they should eat. Basic economic rules like "make good food and get many customers" still apply.)

In the very beginning of all this creation, the need for raw materials presents a challenge. To move ahead with initial construction, we will load materials onto big barges from Brazzaville (the river passing Bangui is navigable during some parts of the year) as well as driving trucks from Cameroon. We will need wood, cement, steel, and materials like doors, wiring, and A/C units. Locals, newly trained as truck drivers, will be given that mission, and they will be paid fairly. One or more of the major freight companies will be urged to establish a central African presence – with them come trucks, international connections, and jobs. And logistics knowledge.

The first building to be raised will be a somewhat massive warehouse. Just a huge temperature-controlled room divided into sections with some cargo bays for trucks and easy access to the newly poured cement ramp. We need space to accept the waves of incoming transport planes and space to store their cargo. Pouring concrete, even just a flat slab, is surprisingly difficult. Drainage, weights, and tensile strength must all be considered. All the same, the work itself will be performed mainly by locals.

Imagine a centrally located "school" teaching all these new skills: a group learning truck driving in one room, while another group learns about modern farming.

Pre-existing skills are much less important than willingness to learn. (Besides, when something goes wrong and a redo is called for, everyone gains in some way. Failures are a natural part of learning, and reaching success without them deprives you of learning opportunities along the way – failing improves you.) The project managers will be experienced teachers and trainers from large Western construction firms. The loading and unloading machinery needed to handle several simultaneous arrivals is readily available on the used market: modern machinery has mainly advanced in automation, reducing the labor needed to run it – shortage of willing laborers is not really a problem in the CAR. Not yet.

At this point, we need to talk about ownership, mainly of buildings and machinery. The buildings are pretty simple: the airport is owned by the government and the buildings are on airport land, so they must be owned by the government. Documents need to be drawn up that let "the project" use the buildings freely but that reverts their control to the government when certain conditions are met. The "things," like machinery and computers, are a different issue. They will probably be owned by the Red Cross or another NGO – to ensure that "the project" does not own anything that has been donated. Avoiding any and all signs of personal enrichment is very important. The project itself cannot be run by an existing NGO – it needs the clean slate start only a new organization can offer.

While the buildings are being raised and the ramp is being paved, we need to ensure that local interaction remains as high and positive as possible without compromising on any modern safety standards, even if that means working at a reduced pace. Construction machinery will likely be supplied by France, not only because of a collective post-colonial poor conscience but primarily because the necessary used equipment is available for a relatively low cost. The upside of a strong CAR to the world in general and to France in particular is obvious, at least to the French. Turning the CAR from a costly bad conscience to a source of wealth, knowledge, and resources would help France greatly. The machinery will be manned by people living in Bangui, probably near the airport. In many cases, it might be the first machine they ever operate. Locally recruited community leaders will themselves recruit the women and men who want to drive an excavator or wheel loader. Yes, training them will be a slow process, and mistakes will be made, but every opportunity for knowledge transfer must be taken. An "adult playground" might be a good idea – a huge fenced area with lots of heavy machines and welcoming instructors. Those interested in learning more advanced techniques can move to simulators. The few buildings in this playground and everywhere else – residential or not – will be quite standardized. Certain types of buildings or rooms might even be modular. Regardless, they require some predefined guidelines, like X number of restrooms for Y expected inhabitants, ventilation, sewage, air conditioning, and universal wheelchair access. Well-established construction regulations will be followed, especially those concerning worker safety. These buildings will perhaps not win any architecture awards, but they will be created with new and modern energy conservation techniques and with safety in mind.

With a warehouse, ramp, and offices in place, we can start accepting cargo. We will first ask the richer countries of the world for water, infant formula, and simple food in sustainable packaging. Sustainable packaging already exists – basically a paper box – but we will go further: the paper of each box should contain some seeds of something locally suitable like okra or palms (The desertification of the north is something that deserves focused attention, but later), preferably something edible that yields quickly. In other words, not asparagus. The influx of aircraft filled with donated basics will almost certainly fill the warehouse. If it doesn't, we will purchase water and infant formula by the ton.

The second phase of providing for basic needs is divided into two parts. It aims to distribute water and formula across the entire country. First, we need to visit the population centers. Bangui is home to much of the population, but not the majority. Most people live rurally or in groups much too small to be considered population centers. Visitors to these areas, preferably arriving by land, will include a CAR resident, a member of the core project group, and a few representatives from Doctors Without Borders (or another secular NGO with an impeccable track record; DWB, however, seems to be somewhat unique in their almost total disregard for anything except helping people. Show me a country with desperate needs and I'll show you a country with a DWB presence). The stated goal will be to ensure that all people have daily access to 1500 mL (or whatever is medically justified) of clean drinking water each, in addition to water for cooking and cleaning. While we are delivering supplies to those close by via road, we will also be performing air drops to those in the CAR far away from Bangui or not accessible by road. We will start as far away as aircraft ranges allow us with the flights and use the ground-based approach to reach those in southern CAR.

For people close to Bangui, we have another trick for immediate water access: mobile water treatment plants. These plants are the size of a semi-tractor trailer and can clean in excess of 500 gallons of water per minute. Not surprisingly, this is an extremely energy-demanding process – but we need potable water and we need it now. Hopefully, one truck pulling one plant can visit several population centers per day – and random points across the countryside. We would fill huge containers for storage. These tanks will use evaporative cooling to keep the contents cold enough to be drinkable. Thankfully, the CAR has access to plenty of water. It is incredibly dirty and practically unusable without some form of treatment, but still, it is there. It is entirely possible that it would be smarter to do purification in Bangui and distribute potable water to outlying areas – someone knowledgeable in supply chain logistics probably knows.

Eventually, of course, water will need be treated on a massive scale in the country. To the north of Bangui is an uninhabited area that would be perfect for a water treatment plant – perfect because it is close to Bangui and because there is space for the solar panels needed to power the plant. And lots of power is needed! Acres of panels, and that will increase as more energy is required. It will work like this: water is taken from the Ubangi river, goes through the treatment plant, and is then pumped up into a water tower (or rather, several towers) that can hold a million gallons each. Creating millions of gallons of drinkable water per day is a relatively easy request from today's modern plants. As nearby villages are ready, they will get their own tower. Using the Ubangi to feed this water treatment plant is smart – the flow in the river is massive: in excess of 800 cubic meters per second. And to start pumping clean water into the countryside for drinking and watering crops is no impossible task either: we humans are good at pipelines.

SAFE AND SOUND

Water is a cornerstone of health in general. Preventing disease demands consistent access. And people everywhere deserve access to the treatments and cures for diseases invented in the last century. Few would quarrel with that. It is not realistic, however, to expect complex organ transplants and other equally advanced procedures to be performed in Bangui from day one. However, delivering a child cannot be allowed to be a chess game with death. In other words, Bangui healthcare needs to be expanded and the levels of hygiene and patient safety need to be increased quite dramatically, beyond even our mercenaries of hygiene. But let's not kid ourselves: healthcare in the developing world is a wheel already invented by Doctors Without Borders and others. What they will probably do is provide many doctors and nurses. We need to supply them with space in a clean – and continually cleaned – building designed by them and give them access to equipment and medicine and sterile tools. Meanwhile, local residents with sufficient education will, both in Bangui Hospital and in a few of the world's leading teaching hospitals (after being sent there), start as observing interns and end up as fully qualified nurses.

Opposite the Bangui hospital – on the other side of a dirt road – is an empty lot. Here we can construct a building with offices and wards – DWB will instruct us in what to build. When they start seeing patients, we will pair DWB's doctors with CAR doctors as much as possible so that each patient meets two doctors. Hopefully, several successful CAR emigrants who have attended medical school and become MDs will move home – or at least help CAR heal for several years. It is unavoidable that some patients, especially initially, will need life-saving procedures that simply cannot be done anywhere in the CAR. These cases must be dealt with smartly. Luckily, transport aircraft bringing essential supplies to CAR will be leaving practically empty, and they are almost all designed to carry people on stretchers who are in need of medical supervision. The procedures needed will mostly be of a basic nature to a Western doctor with Western support – so independent of whether the procedures are donated, they will not break the bank.

To raise the floor for hygiene across Bangui, we will place tens (then, with time, hundreds) of mobile restrooms and showers around the city. These mobile hygiene stations will all be cleaned and disinfected daily by well-supplied – and well-paid – local cleaners.

Speaking of hygiene, a sibling to the water treatment plant is a waste treatment plant. In fact, great benefit can be drawn from building the two as one plant. Hyper-modern technology allows the creation of potable water from waste, but this includes too many risks (not to mention the yuck factor). The plant itself and the batteries needed to power it will be north of the city – the necessary energy will be generated by shared solar panels centrally located between the plant and the city. The cement tubes and pumps needed to move waste from Bangui are bulky, so they will be brought in by sea and barge – and remember: months have passed by now. The infrastructure to support this growth should be in place.

There is already a dock in Bangui for boats, if we use the term dock very loosely, on the river. A modern harbor – with cranes, chutes for grain, pumps and hoses for liquids, and container-handling facilities – needs to be built eventually. However, local capacity and capability will be much improved with just a slab and a crane or two. We must assume that several sizable ships and barges will always be there loading or unloading. Initially, barges will be used to dredge the river, making it deep enough to support year-round access by large vessels. Brazzaville is already reachable almost the entire year via the Ubangi and Congo rivers, and from Brazzaville, trains take us to the Atlantic coast of Africa, in Pointe-Noire. This is important because of simple math. The tonnage numbers are comically different when comparing cargo via air with cargo via sea and rail. An airplane can carry 20–70 metric tons of cargo; a barge can carry 1500 tons. And a *single rail car* carries 100 tons. Imagine a super long train... Connecting Bangui to a rail system with coastal access will be a priority. But later.

Usage of the waste plant obviously depends on households being connected to it. Obviously, being connected depends on a physical connection between the treatment plant and houses via sewer pipes. When we dig to lay these pipes, we will at the same time lay pipes for fresh water and empty pipes for future expansions. Connecting these pipes to houses will require general contracting and plumbing. Getting a planeload of WCs and sinks will not be particularly difficult – they are neither rare nor expensive. Getting qualified plumbers with knowledge of trenching, however, might be difficult, but not impossible. Along with WCs we will start bringing in toilet paper. This will be available for no charge, and as a result, the distribution points within Bangui will now have water, formula, nutrition, a shower, a bathroom, and toilet paper.

A somewhat sneaky part of the general effort to increase public cleanliness is done with the help of basketball, the most popular physical recreation in the CAR. Despite its popularity, there are surprisingly few courts in the country. This needs to change. We will ask a few of the professionally successful CAR-born basketball players will be the face of a project that builds many courts and – crucially

– changing rooms with showers. There are companies who, with the right equipment, need only days to build a high-quality court. We need to get the population of Bangui to have fun, to move, and to shower.

REACHING THE SEA

The country of Cameroon lies directly west of the CAR. To the west of Cameroon is something we desperately need access to: the Atlantic Ocean. As opposed to the CAR, Cameroon has its own railway with one end, of course, on the coast. Connecting the CAR in general and Bangui in particular to this network has been discussed for years, and rightly so: it would bring massive positive change. The best place to start is probably in the city of Bélabo, almost due west of Bangui. Wisely implemented, such a rail network could be fantastic. Emissions are low per ton hauled – even if the train is powered by diesel. Risks are low, and massive amounts of cargo can be carried quickly. *Can*. When done wrong, however, rail transport can be a quagmire of problems. Even though this might be, at face value, a simple rail line, there are several huge challenges: flooding, wildlife, and public safety, to mention a few. Because this line must operate year-round to ensure consistent access to the Atlantic, it must be completely flood-resistant. Well, to a point: we have neither time nor funds to completely protect it from everything all the time. The simplest solution is to elevate the tracks. I do not mean build a bridge, but rather an embankment with lots of tunnels through it for use by humans and wildlife. That being said, every mile or so, the rail line will be elevated on a long, relatively low bridge – tall enough for things like a herd of giraffe to pass. These embankments will be relatively wide, and the sides will not be steep. To further ensure safety, the tracks will be fenced. The side of the embankment will have a high-quality two-way road.

This rail line needs to be built rather quickly: 200 men in three shifts building from both ends would do it. And for the first (and hopefully only) time, we need to focus on speed. Some Asian countries have become masters of mind-bogglingly fast infrastructure projects. A team from China will probably need around 100 days to lay the 500 km of powered, high-quality double track that are needed. China has emerged as the absolute world leader in rail technology. Naturally, CAR engineers and laborers will observe, but in the name of speed, most of the active work will be done by the Chinese.

When the line is complete and trains are purchased, we are again faced with the challenge of ownership. Because the airport will be owned by the government, it is tempting to let them own the railway as well. This presents two problems based on the fact that the rail system will be worth millions: the government has been an active combatant in recent civil wars, so, first, enriching them will not be universally popular, and second, it would be direct funding of armed conflict. An obvious option is handing ownership over to one of the large NGOs. However, Amnesty International and other NGOs are assuredly not really interested in entering the central African rail business. One of the primary goals of this project is to ensure that the CAR becomes a strong, self-governing democracy. Therefore, the rails and trains must be CAR-controlled, at least eventually. A non-profit could be formed which, when certain criteria are met, will fully hand over all control to a third organization independent of the government. Meanwhile, the bylaws of the NPO will direct all profits (assuming the cost of building is carried elsewhere) into further infrastructure development. Maybe high speed. Maybe connecting to Cairo and/or Johannesburg.

TRAINS, PLANES, AND AUTOMOBILES

Intra-country infrastructure is particularly poor in the CAR, and that causes issues. Even with a rail connection to Cameroon, the CAR would rank among the worst countries in the world with regard to infrastructure. Not only are almost all roads unpaved and impassable during flood season, but there is no domestic train system and practically no domestic air service. The lack of physical mobility hinders social mobility. But this can all change.

The CAR is in possession of 38 flight runways of various lengths. Of these, approximately 36 can be used by semi-modern one-engine aircraft. That is a lot: we might start with only one plane and a handful of pilots and the goal of visiting each airport once weekly. The Cessna Caravan, for example, has only one engine and is certified for single-pilot operation. While a used Cessna will cost hundreds of thousands of dollars, we must put this cost into perspective: a commercial jetliner built in Seattle or Toulouse might cost hundreds of *millions* of dollars and have a wait list of years. Instead, we can spend a thousand times less and get the plane delivered within a week. This service will be folded into the existing official airline, Karinou Airlines – a small CAR-based airline with 10 (*ish*) international destinations and no domestic service. As the big brother of this new service, Karinou will have additional benefits: a super thing about the Caravan being certified for single-pilot use is that a second person can sit in the cockpit and learn to fly it. Soon, the sky will be filled with planes flown by highly qualified Central Africans. Moving heavier and bulkier items, however, is not possible by small commuter plane. For that, we need roads that are usable by heavy trucks all year long. In other words, roads need to be quite flood-resistant. Because there are already roads, we already know where they must be. The existing roads are not anywhere near top quality, but this is not about renewing the roads, it is about redoing them from scratch. The new roads must be slightly elevated, and the drainage must be world class. Despite the cost and the speed penalties incurred, the roads of the CAR will be paved with concrete rather than asphalt due to the better durability of concrete in warm environments, and the work will be done by locals. With several teams working around the clock, we could aim for 10 km of daily paving after a few months of training. A paving crew doesn't need to be particularly large – instead we will have lots of crews working at once. The roads to be paved will initially all originate in Bangui. When the closest cities are connected, we will connect those cities to each other before we connect additional cities to our growing network. Existing roads in Bangui have names, but there is no consistent signage, so we will simply copy a successful and clear system: it has been said that Canada has signage that is particularly good. Signage will be tri-lingual: all signs will be in Sangho, French, and English.

Next to many of these roads, we will construct rail. As with the connection to Cameroon, rail lines will be raised and fenced, interspersed now and then with long bridges to allow animals and humans to pass. As opposed to the rail line headed west, the speed with which these rail lines are built is not priority number one. This is a perfect opportunity to further local training of construction crews supervised by the Chinese. When we are laying rail, we should also lay optical fiber – or something else – to prepare for some sort of data transfer (probably for telecommunications), just as we did while trenching for power to the light posts for the roads.

We must also expand the Bangui train station. Even though the system will, at first, be quite small, the station needs quite a lot of platforms to prepare for future growth. And there must be a separate freight loading and unloading section! The rail network must be prepared for both regional and international travel – the airport shows that the CAR already understands the formalities of international travel and passports and visas.

To use all these new ways of transport, we will, along with obtaining many used aircraft and trains, focus on helping the road transport industry. This will be done by subsidizing purchases of trucks and busses with micro-loans. A public transport system will hopefully be started, at least in Bangui. We will not start it directly as part of the project; it will emerge together with taxi services started by independent Central Africans as a result of new demand. Citizens and visitors alike will be able to quickly move themselves or things around the CAR.

This expansion of the infrastructure is, of course, a massive project, and it's one that never really ends – upkeep is as important as building it in the first place. The job of keeping infrastructure networks safe and in great shape never ceases. And it's an endeavor that can employ a lot of people. As crews gain skills, other countries might start contracting them for jobs somewhere else entirely.

POWER TO THE PEOPLE

A country speeding through development like the CAR is doing now consumes a lot of energy. And one of the many natural resources with which the CAR is blessed is sunlight – lots of sunlight. This means that creating solar energy "farms" is a pretty wise idea. Even though the space and technology are available to create such a farm very simply that could power the entire country (space-wise the one now active in Hawaii would be several times too large), we will at this stage create energy only for Bangui and its new, inflated energy consumption. The first farm will power the cleaning of water and waste. Power will go into a series of huge batteries, which in turn will power the city, the water cleaning plant, the sewage treatment plant, and the trains. The batteries will probably hold ten or so times the average amount of electricity used daily so that rainy days will not cause outages. One of the many magnificent aspects of solar energy is the ease of expansion: when Bangui starts consuming more and more energy, the solar farm simply grows. A single train could bring in thousands of solar panels, enough to cover even the biggest thinkable increase in consumption. Power transport from the solar farm to the city will be redundant and underground. More than one massive cable will be laid in new sole-use trenches dug at different depths. (Trenches for power need to be separate from other trenches – the power trenches must, for example, be significantly deeper.) For trenches around town, simple tractor attachments are powerful enough to get the job done. But we are talking about a ditch 2 m deep, 20 cm wide, and 20 km long, so we need to bring in the big guns. Trenching machines will be necessary. These machines look crazy – like a huge slow-moving chainsaw sawing the ground. All the work done trenching must be written down and photographed. Documentation, although dreadfully boring, is very important: we need to know where not to dig in the future.

Ownership and cost remain a challenge. One is tempted to yell "free power," but that is likely not the best long-term approach. (Rather the opposite. The artificially low cost of energy in Venezuela has not really worked as intended. Mass starvation, dictatorship, and societal collapse are not particularly pleasant goals.) Eventually, there must be a cost, so introducing one now – albeit only paid only by those who can afford to – is likely wise. Maybe we can say "all businesses pay per kw/h (including, of course, the businesses created by the project) and households with a monthly income over X pay a token flat fee," or something similar. This policy will likely mean hundreds of thousands of households wanting electricity, which in turn means that trench digging and electrical installation must happen on an intense scale. Luckily (well...), roads in Bangui are almost all unpaved, so trenching will be relatively pain free. Besides, trenches will be beside the road, so even where roads are already paved, we can move forward. A network of cables will branch out from several backbones, which in turn will connect to the main line coming from the solar farm, almost like the arteries of a body. Connection points will mostly be above ground in the types of locked electrical boxes that we are used to seeing in the West. Or rather, the ones that are so prevalent that we don't see them at all. But these connection points have additional purposes. When we lay wires for electricity, we will also lay fiberoptic lines and empty conduits for future technologies.

PERCEIVED SAFETY

Now that the most essential human needs are dealt with in Bangui, we need to ensure that people feel physically safe. For example, there must be a widespread feeling of safety when walking outside in the dark, especially for the group of people that will likely lead the CAR into better times: the women. For this, there must first be light. And Bangui is dark. Well, at night I mean: the combination of no street lighting and the non-universal dissemination of electricity makes nighttime in Bangui very dark and somewhat scary. This needs to change, and it can. The question really is just where to begin, and the answer is pretty self-explanatory: start in the center. The center of Bangui is aptly called City Center and is a roundabout connecting six roads, two of which are the city's main roads. We will begin by lighting these two roads: RN6 and Avenue de l'Independance. But using what? Modern poles might look like the poles of old, but almost nothing else is the same. No metal, no light-bulbs. This is the age of composites and LEDs. The removal of metal increases strength, lowers weight, dramatically lowers environmental impact, and does – or rather does not do – one more important thing: the pole no longer conducts electricity. In an application like this, where it is likely to be touched often, increased public safety is greatly appreciated. LEDs, as opposed to traditional lightbulbs, draw much less electricity and have an enormously long expected life, something like 60,000 hours. That is 12 hours per day, every day, for over 13 years.

But safety goes further than streetlights. People need a visible and clearly uncorrupt police. Or rather, people need *someone* who absolutely, positively is not corrupt and who can always be trusted. The CAR has a policing system based – at least once upon a time

– on the French system: one civilian arm and one military arm. CAR policing has for many years lacked sufficient resources, like money for salaries, and officers who don't get paid still need to feed their children, so they get money elsewhere. Corruption is rarely caused by calculating and evil people – the root cause is almost always pure desperation. Police in the CAR have experienced their fair share of desperate situations. In other words, confidence in the police is severely compromised, and few things are as difficult to regain once lost as trust. So, instead of trying only to reestablish trust in the police, something else is needed as well.

How about a group modeled on the New York citizen patrol, the civilian Guardian Angels, with some significant differences? Members of this new patrol could walk around, would be highly visible, and would be tasked with doing good. They could be called the Bangui Help, and it would be a paid job. Members of the group would wear matching uniforms to make them easily recognizable, and they would significantly outnumber the police – not particularly difficult, as there are only ~1000 police officers in a country with a population of ~5 million. The BH will be constantly visible and unarmed. Many will be women. This is where the optical fiber lines in the electricity boxes come in – each box will have a "phone" with only one button calling only one number – a central Bangui call center in contact with the Bangui Help. There would be thousands of such phones. When the button is pressed, the call will be answered, a BH patrol will be directed to the phone's location, and assistance will be given. No matter whether someone wants company walking home or a scuffle needs to be stopped, the BH will be there for almost everything: serious crime will remain a police issue. While the BH is ramping up, we need to invest in the reputation of the official CAR police. We need to ensure that they are well compensated, well equipped, and visible. Perhaps most importantly, they must be motivated. Walking pairs of trained and happy officers will be everywhere. Large fleets of police vehicles will be brought in and Bangui will with relative haste become the safest capital in Africa.

Physical safety can also be increased with a well-equipped and well-trained fire department. Trucks and gear discarded as old in the United States is a thousand times better than nothing at all. With some experienced instructors, Bangui can have top-flight fire protection manned by equitably paid Central Africans. By now, we even have a source for clean and safe water for use in the fire trucks – muddy, dirty river water is not good for fire truck pumps.

For all of this to work at all, women need to be empowered, if for no other reason than to double the workforce. Empowering women must be done in steps. The first step is security in the form of full control of their own bodies – namely, access to quality women's health facilities. Women are so systematically oppressed in most developing nations that they probably will not just come by themselves: women are seen as property. And that needs to stop. We will begin by building women's health clinics. These smallish but well disseminated facilities will not offer or perform invasive procedures, but they will be stocked with contraceptives, hygiene products, and an empowering message. All visitors will also be given the opportunity to request micro-credit and will be given a bag of seeds if they desire. These facilities will be manned solely by women from the CAR and a volunteer women's health professional, and it will be – naturally – completely anonymous.

THE CAR CAR

One of the major difficulties in offering high-quality healthcare in a poorly developed area is not knowing who is who, which can be very important for reasons including follow-up, doctor instructions and prescription medicine. People who don't know their own exact age, who have no education, and who may not even have clean water to drink probably don't have a passport.

Enter technology.

In the United States, everyone has a social security number. Swedes have an ID number based on their day of birth. Throughout the Western world, most people have a number – a number that generally (in theory) is known only to you and to which almost all information about you is tied. But this is somewhat old-fashioned – such analog systems come with the real possibility of identities being stolen, resulting in financial disasters or false voting or any one of many other awful outcomes. There are companies around that are trying to deal with this. One way is to connect a person to their fingerprint. Another way is to connect them to their irises. But these things might change with time, and it can hardly be guaranteed that all people will always have fingers or eyes. Losing a hand in an accident, for example, can't be allowed to result in lost medical history, and equating limb-theft with identity-theft seems risky. The answer must be DNA. It must be gathered in a non-invasive way – a country full of needles is not really what we need. Some innovation is needed here: building a complete DNA profile today takes weeks, and we need it done in under a minute. Well, we may not need a complete profile – only one that is sufficiently complete to ensure that one person is who he or she says. Integrity must be at the tip of our tongue: the DNA database will be off limits to almost all: perhaps especially to the police. There will be many loud calls to give access to certain entities – such requests and demands must always be denied (access to medical information is solely for medical professionals, etc.), even when faced with morally and ethically challenging questions. There must be no hesitation from the public to want to join the Central Africans' Register. Doctors and really anyone with a mobile scanner could add people to the CAR CAR. Vehicles used to visit villages will bring along their own mobile WiFi hotspot so that scans will be saved directly to the computer in the car to be synced later with the main system. Maybe a name or age or blood type will be added – and maybe not. Or maybe a picture, or blood pressure, or temperature.

Ideally, the register will be physically located somewhere in the Central African Republic. Alas, the offerings for triple redundant servers with minute-by-minute incremental backups are quite slim in central Africa. Luckily, these services are readily available elsewhere. Data will be strongly and securely encrypted and copied over the whole world to ensure redundancy and immediate worldwide access. (Encryption done right simply can't be broken, physically. Even if you use all the computers on earth, a solution would still not be found for millions of years.) The registry will be used for storing practically everything, although daily access to certain section might not require a DNA test. Of equal importance is where and when it is *not* used. Contraceptives, for example, will be available without registry involvement. And it the registry should not be used as a paternity test.

Such a registry could expand quite quickly. Imagine 50 or so vehicles driving across the country doing scans on everyone they meet (everyone who allows it). Still, even if it grows at an impressive pace, the registry will not be completed overnight. The CAR is, after all, a country of around 5 million people. It should be noted, though, that the process of adding someone to the Registry really doesn't demand any skills and never gives access to any classified information; the job of traveling the countryside and scanning might be a tempting job for both volunteers and Central Africans. And who knows: there might not be 50 concurrently operating scanners: there might be 500. As this database grows and fills with sensitive information, its value will increase quickly. Because the database is originally intended to aid in providing medical care, it is tempting to place ownership with the hospital. But doctors are generally not great administrators and are rarely tech-savvy. It is important to note that all info within the registry is ultimately owned by the person in question – responsibility for the registry in no way gives access to the information contained within. Administrative ownership only deals with issues like giving people access to their own files or expanding the registry to include video or developing the system with time. Administrative ownership is likely to be the state's, supported by a group of up-to-date IT engineers.

PAUSE AND REFLECT

So, where are we? First, we need to remember where we started: the CAR is one of the poorest countries in the world, and it faces huge challenges in terms of corruption and starvation, not to mention the medical problems. Some of these challenges will remain at this point – perhaps mainly malaria – but we will have solved many challenges, more or less. Fewer and fewer people are faced with starvation and malnutrition. There is a rail connection to Cameroon. Movement of people, goods, and ideas has increased. There is water, sanitation, and physical security in Bangui, and tens of thousands more people are working for fair pay and even more have new skills. Hotels are booked and the restaurants are filled as never before. There are many basketball courts, and everyone is near a shower and a clean WC. Public dumping of garbage and waste has practically ceased. The city is at long last well lit. And it is growing! People are moving in large numbers to the jobs and healthcare and safety of Bangui.

But most importantly: women are being empowered. They are applying for, and getting, micro-loans to start businesses. Women are being treated well medically – they are the captains of their own lives. Women are lifting CAR upwards.

Cost? Well, lots. Tens of millions of dollars, certainly. But, at the risk of sounding a bit disconnected: it isn't *that* much. Around 25 countries each spend over a billion US dollars yearly on developmental foreign aid. And as opposed to some of the obscure projects that are being funded right now, we will have saved hundreds of lives in front of the eyes of the world.

But arguably, the most interesting changes are the ones we have *not* brought. Like the movement of people towards cities and the emergence of many new companies – some of which have in turn created jobs. Thanks to the availability of space and clean water, some have used micro-loans to create huge agricultural farms, growing things not only for the CAR but – with the rail network in place and with all these transport aircraft – for export. However, the single most significant change is this: *people have hope*. Smiles are everywhere, and thoughts about the future are excited and positive.

The availability of micro-loans and the existence of well-seasoned construction crews have likely resulted in an explosion of small hotels, with an emphasis on small: one or two room hostels are probably the norm. But now, a strong business case exists for hotel chains, especially chains targeting with fewer guests who are less price-sensitive. Like adventure safari resorts. The opportunity to dine alongside wildlife will surely be a draw.

All resorts in the CAR must be eco-friendly and must focus on conservation. Luckily, most luxury chains already have this profile. In fact, they will probably lead the task of creating national parks and wildlife reserves, as well as documenting wildlife.

Gladly, poaching – and hunting in general – will quickly end, not only because more people will be moving around the countryside but also because the economic incentives will no longer be there. Getting an honest job is not challenging. There is still work to be done, however, and the CAR understands the value of a healthy environment, so hundreds of rangers are employed by the state.

The new attractions are not limited to land either. Boat rides and "canal cruises" are a great way of both showing off the country and spreading tourist money. Ultimately, visitors spend money and create demand for new things.

Along with this influx of wealth will come banks, some local, many international. Bangui is becoming so significant indeed that some banks with only one African office place that office here. The CAR capital is, after all, connected with all of Africa and with the world, and its university produces more than enough quality graduates to meet employment needs.

In all likelihood, we could end this experiment right here and now. We have set in motion natural forces of development that are unlikely to slow. The Central African Republic will continue to grow and will continue to improve in all sorts of important ways. In fact, in many ways, the CAR already has – rankings of GDP and such have drastically improved. But we can't stop now. There are many reasons, including (but not limited to) all the opportunities that are available and the relative ease with which many of these opportunities may be taken advantage of. Healthcare must still be better. Some women still feel forced to have child after child: their deliveries must be top notch. And we need to increase the mobility of people and goods within the CAR and the region. Infrastructure needs to improve in the capital, and we must begin broader national dissemination of water and waste treatment to rural areas. We must aid farmers in growing and selling crops or animals. And we must educate the CAR – illiteracy is still widespread. There are also some environmental challenges ahead. The CAR also needs to have something to export that everybody needs, something that capitalizes on what the CAR already has.

DISPENSING JUICE

Africa is a continent that is in many ways behind, say, Europe. In practically every way, the Western world is ahead of Africa. But there is at least one clear exception: most of Africa's land mass is closer to the equator than most of the Western world, and the continent has lots of open land. Lack of land creates challenges for countries like the Netherlands; in contrast, the prevalence of open land in the CAR can be used to great benefit. Exports from the CAR today are dominated by raw materials: uncut diamonds, timber, or coffee beans, to mention a few. What they all have in common is quite obvious: extraction or production that leaves lasting scars on the environment and the people. Wounds have for hundreds of years been cut into Africa by Westerners with little concern – those times need to be over. Exports from the CAR of tomorrow will be renewable and will be made from the most abundant resource in Sub-Saharan Africa: sunlight. The potential for solar power is mind boggling. Renewable energy is not a new idea in this part of the world. Somewhat progressively, the CAR has three hydroelectric power plants, but the country still burns close to 2000 barrels of oil per day just to satisfy domestic energy demand. Some oil will need to be imported for the foreseeable future: in fact, imports of gasoline, diesel, and jet fuel will probably increase with increased development. But the vast majority of oil use can simply be replaced. The only real resource needed for solar panels is space – tens of acres, eventually hundreds, and possibly even more. We will have panels and we will have batteries. And perhaps most tantalizing, solar farms work best in environments that humans shun. Too hot and dry? Soil infertile? Perfect for a solar farm.

Overall, we aim to make the CAR both energy independent and a major supplier of electricity in Africa. This will be accomplished by focusing on domestic demand first. We will start with one quite massive solar farm. It already powers a water treatment plant, a waste treatment plant, a rail network, and a city. It must grow considerably – in terms of both solar power panels and batteries. Solar energy can obviously not be harvested at night, but energy demand hardly disappears with the sun – quite the opposite. So, the panels must charge the batteries while also meeting current demand.

How about exports? Well, the two countries with exceptional energy consumption in Africa are Egypt and South Africa. Because these two countries are at opposite ends of the continent, connecting the CAR grid to only one of them at a time makes sense. Electricity in Egypt is quite heavily government subsidized, while in South Africa, it is not. That being said, to the north lie several other mid-level consumers: mainly Algeria, Morocco, Tunisia, and Libya (who all probably should build solar farms of their own, but who also fear the initial costs). The distances are almost equal, but the areas to the north of CAR are mostly desert, and several energy firms in the Middle East have become masters at desert labor. Getting paid can be easier than imagined – we let local and national companies deal with end users and simply sell electricity to a big existing provider. It's not as simple as placing a cable from our sun farm to their grid, installing a meter and signing some papers, but it's not much more difficult. To ensure that all steps are immediately made profitable, the first phase will go northwest through Cameroon to Nigeria. We can use cables buried while laying rail, supplemented by cables on towers through the desert.

It is important that the energy production revenues go to the country itself. For the first couple of years, almost all profit will go towards expansion – of the farm itself as well as of the different markets serviced. Eventually, this energy company will be huge, and it will generate enormous amounts of money for the CAR, money that can be used to continue making the country a better place.

NOT TOO COOL FOR SCHOOL

In many ways, the CAR is a country of contrasts. Those on the bottom are really at the bottom. People are not "economically challenged" – they are dying! And the fact that the capital actually has some healthcare facilities – albeit poor – right now skews the published averages. In some villages, a quarter of all births result in the death of the woman or of the child within five years. Bringing people in general and women in particular up from this swamp of pain and suffering demands among other things some education. Schooling really is the beginning of a trip out of starvation and hopelessness: the feeling of liberation that comes with becoming literate cannot be downplayed. For education to become widespread, we need, in order of increasing difficulty: buildings, teachers, and students. The project already possesses knowledge of quick, safe, and sustainable building. And by now, local contractors have become masters. Concrete can be transported to the CAR via Cameroon by rail, and smaller, lighter things like chalk and erasers can enter the country via air. Establishing a building with several classrooms and filling it with school materials is just the beginning. Finding teachers will be a major challenge, not only because good teachers are rare but also because this type of teaching is so different: many of these classes will focus on very basic literacy. And at times, the students will be significantly older than the teacher. This is actually good: everybody needs to learn about the concept of everyone's equal worth and about general humanism. Also, teachers in the West *generally* love teaching and making a difference, while the CAR does not have the luxury of a motivated department of education. Luckily, skilled administrators exist, and they tend to really be engaged when it comes to providing basic education. A central governing board will make decisions to ensure that education in the CAR is consistent, tested, and of high quality. Eventually this governing board will be folded into the government, but not until a certain set of criteria have been met.

This leaves the biggest challenge: students. We should not shy away from the fact that we, in many cases, are asking people to part with ancient traditions or cultural beliefs, or worst of all: spiritual convictions. Some people actually believe that some invisible man in the sky doesn't want girls to read. But there are few things as vital as getting these children to school, even if it means bribing the parents (or the children). These children are destined to inherit a country much different from the one in which they grew up: education will be of utmost importance.

M'POKO LOVE

As the name gently hints, the Central African Republic is located in central Africa. It is roughly equidistant from all ends of the continent. It is not far from Dubai, which in turn is only one flight from just about anywhere. The CAR is, in other words, perfectly placed for hosting a regional African airline.

However, M'Poko is pretty far from being as perfect, not only compared to airports in the West but also compared to many other African airports. Perimeter integrity is practically nonexistent and there is a huge lack of services necessary to support tens (or many more) of daily flights. The gaps are large enough that one is tempted to think about a new airport – a do-over, getting it right this time. But there is barely anything in the world of construction as complex as building a brand-new airport. There are inevitably cost and time overruns. Think tens of years and billions of dollars. In other words: let's keep the current airport and give M'Poko some TLC.

The first challenge is fencing and perimeter enforcement. This needs to be done delicately, as those still living on airport property are mostly internally displaced refugees. However, this offers one quite large advantage: they know the language. And we already have housing for them! This is their country. We mustn't fall into the classic trap of moving everybody to the same place at once. The business of creating a ghetto is one business we won't enter. Luckily, Bangui is not lacking space to expand into and we have become quite proficient at quickly creating small homes. With M'Poko cleared, we need to reinforce security, patrol the grounds, and put alarms on the fence. When it comes to air travel, especially for flights to and from Europe and the United States, security on the ground is incredibly important. This means that after fencing, we must with equal rigor introduce badges for the people who actually *should* be there. This will probably include some new construction of entrances and security checkpoints. Upgrading much else is somewhat pointless without passengers, with one huge exception: emergency services. Luckily the second-hand market for things like airport fire trucks is huge: almost everybody seems to want to upgrade for more automation. That is hardly our focus – we want to create jobs, not automate them away.

But, as we noted earlier, the CAR is perfectly placed for serving Africa. And the second-hand market for airliners is also huge. A handful of people in the world have become immensely proficient at turning this type of situation into a massive success. Niki Lauda is arguably the best – if we give him a handful of aircraft, an updated hub, and a general plan, we will have a successful and growing airline within a few years, I am certain. He would probably even do it without being offered fantasy-sum levels of compensation.

PAUSE AND REFLECT AGAIN

A few years have gone by now, and the CAR is a completely different country than it was when we began. And the improvements have spread far from Bangui. One of the major improvements making an obvious and highly visible difference is the new infrastructure. Rail, road, and air combine to connect practically all citizens of the CAR with the rest of the world. More importantly, however, it facilitates the free movement of ideas and skills within the country. Ways to improve crop yields or ideas about how to start a business are shared practically overnight. Information that improves lives has a wide and rapid reach. Not only does this make the country more productive but it also makes the country significantly healthier. Life expectancy has risen dramatically, and childbirth is no longer feared. Malaria is no longer the leading cause of death, and genital mutilation is, thank goodness, a thing of the past. Education and health-care access do wonders.

The desertification of the northern parts of the country has started to reverse itself. The CAR is carbon-negative. With knowledge of relevant flora and access to clean water, planting of new trees has practically exploded in an effort to retake land lost to the Sahara. The countryside in general is greener, more alive. People seem environmentally aware. The water container seeds have done their job.

True democracy has found the CAR. A series of internationally observed elections have been held with a dwindling number of problems. Democracy is doing so well, in fact, that many parts of the project have already been handed over to government ownership. The CAR has control of a continent-covering modern rail system and has the biggest solar energy farm in the southern hemisphere. The energy created roughly matches domestic consumption, but it increases almost daily. Export of energy on a small scale has begun. Export of crops and handmade goods, however, is already significant.

Classrooms across the country are steadily filled with more and more students. The Bangui University is at absolute capacity, and many citizens seek education abroad and hurry home to be a part of this transformation. The school is growing – they probably even offer CAR history classes. Citizens educated in other parts of the world have been coming home. They start many new (to the CAR) types of businesses – like cafés and movie theaters. And they motivate others: literacy has spread like wildfire. Everyone is proud.

People from around the whole region are moving to Bangui. It has become the main hub of central Africa, with flights to the whole world, and it has a prosperous aura, full of curiosity and energy. This movement of people creates demand for things like restaurants and hotels, which in turn creates jobs, which creates movement of people in an ongoing and hugely positive feedback loop. With the influx of people and the easy access to basketball courts the CAR has become a force to be reckoned with in all international basketball tournaments they enter.

For all intents and purposes, we are done here and now. The CAR is quickly becoming a leading country in the region, and all the surrounding countries have started their own development. With better access to water, power, crops, knowledge, and travel, Northern Africa has in its entirety become a better place to be.

But more yet can be done. Much can still be improved. Even though the CAR is happier than ever, it still lacks some things we in the West consider essential. With a few extra steps, the country can move lightyears ahead.

FIGARO IN SWAN LAKE

If there is anything as odd (maybe only to me) as the incredibly positive effect on a population of culture, I don't know about it. But it can't be denied. Be it opera, ballet, or graffiti, art makes those exposed to it better in practically every conceivable way. (Be it national pride around a sports team or an improved family dynamic caused by doing things together culture always betters a society.) This seeming force of nature must be embraced by the CAR. In Sweden, some quite important museums are state-owned and free for all to visit, for the benefit of the whole population. Making culture easily accessible like that is important. The quickest way might be to create a "walk-in" theatre showing important movies nightly. Maybe one theater will specifically show only material suitable for children. The immediate benefits of social interaction will pale in comparison to the long-term gains that come with exposure to culture.

Then we need galleries. A gallery is basically just an empty room with a high ceiling and superb lighting. The challenge at first will probably be getting artists to display their work. With time, their shyness will fade. Naturally, established artists are welcome to apply – appreciation of art knows no language barriers.

A main central building with a stage (and top-notch acoustics) should be built that supports things like a choir or an orchestra or an opera. Getting really good amateur productions will not be difficult. Maybe even an A-list singer will want to perform! In conjunction with the stage, we should see the appearance of a Bangui School of Art. This school will not only have traditional bachelor's degree programs but also offer one-off evening courses that allow people from all walks of life to paint or sculpt or play an instrument.

Significantly less glamourous but possibly more important, we will need well-stocked and active libraries. Libraries have, for some odd reason, become rare in developed nations – whole book collections are locked up and stored away. So, collecting books – in multiple languages – will not be a battle. Good librarians are rare, but – of extra importance here – encouraging reading, which librarians do, brings only good, for example, curiosity and a thirst for further knowledge. And few places are as good at quenching that thirst as a well-curated museum. At first there might only be traveling exhibits, but eventually, the CAR will have permanent museums of things like natural history or modern art. Or sport. But a city with a sports museum must have a state-of-the-art stadium – modern but available to all. It should have lots of basketball courts as well as several soccer pitches and dressing rooms. Bangui already has a stadium, but the nicest thing one can say about it is "nice location." Subpar facilities tend to enjoy subpar utilization.

JUSTICE FOR ALL

Although the CAR has become a relatively peaceful country, law and order must be enforced. A first step is a strong constitution. Perhaps the CAR should copy the French *Constitution of the Fifth Republic*. It is a relatively new document that allows amendments.

With significant knowledge of human rights in general and the new constitution in particular, unarmed policemen and police-women will start patrolling first Bangui and then the countryside. Some of the great countries of the world have unarmed police – even though armed response teams always stand by. Studies have shown that a visible police force brings much good beyond just reducing crime, so high-visibility uniforms are important. The police must be able to drop off suspects in the care of a humane and modern jail. Much can be deduced about a country by the way they treat their prisoners and suspects. So, rather counterintuitively, in a country where we are introducing freedom, we must renovate jails and prisons. An example of a country with a jail system where human rights are the first priority is Norway. The CAR prison system will be based on the Norwegian system, and at first perhaps even run by Norwegians. Some might complain about treating "monsters" well. First, the vast majority of people are *not* monsters. Second, any state must treat everyone humanely, especially those with whom it disagrees.

Before people move from jails to prisons, they must by definition be sentenced. But by whom? And where? This highlights another problem entirely: the lack of government buildings in Bangui. A central spot should be selected where future growth is possible, as a complex of buildings emerges, it will contain several courtrooms that are open to the public. Perhaps this calls for a worldwide architecture competition!

Along with a police force, the CAR should have a well-equipped military. Not that the CAR intends to go to war – the military promotes social and economic mobility and creates national pride, both of which we want. A military also provides jobs and lots of education – there are very few drawbacks. One of the main areas of focus for the military will be the ongoing disarming and reintegration of rebels. This will probably never really end, and it will be costly. But people won't come to the CAR if the chance of death is high, so it is clearly a worthwhile investment.

THE GOOD, THE BAD, AND THE UGLY

Modern society has some elements that are (at least partially) controversial ethically and indeed morally but that will likely never go away: like bars, and clubs, and discos. A strong argument can be made that alcohol, along with tobacco, does so much harm that it should be banned alongside cocaine and heroin. However, society in general seems accepting of alcohol and tobacco – but funds intended to help Africans can't really be used to start a pub. At least not without some serious moral relativism. (We will not even peek at the Pandora's box of marijuana legalization. That might be a fun challenge for the newly appointed high – pun not intended – court.)

Religious buildings are another example of something that can never be directly financed by the project. Not only is the project secular, but history has shown that "religious values" are, to put it incredibly kindly, overrated. One of the most Christian countries *in the world* is Rwanda. The scars in our collective souls from the Rwandan genocide will never completely heal, nor should they. That said, places of worship are welcome but will not receive any taxation benefits. Casinos and gambling are tricky. I think that overall they do more harm than good, but the influx of money and people cannot be ignored. This is a question for government – donated funds will not in any way facilitate gambling.

There will also be regulations in place to govern things like natural resource extraction and excessive advertising. The goal of multinational companies should not be to callously gain millions of new customers and billions of dollars. For example, billboards will be allowed, but in smaller numbers than in the West, and maybe they all will contain cell towers. There will be some significant land owners. Even though they can in essence do what they want on their property, advertising regulations should probably override that right. Larger farms can actually be a thing of beauty if managed correctly. And the food they produce is important for long-term sustainability. But sowing in wholly untouched ground is virtually impossible: for years, farmers will need to engage the ground and make hundreds of acres ready for planting. This may be visually ugly in the near term, but it must be done.

THE END OF THE BEGINNING

Looking back, what have we accomplished and at what price? On a purely material level, lots has happened – the list is long. And it is in this list that we will find some practically guaranteed results of this idea. Schools will exist. Clean water will be available. Healthcare will be relatively modern and wholly safe. The country is, at the very least, energy independent. CAR residents will be connected to the world. And they are all filled with joy, pride, and hope. This is all doable now.

The cost? Lots. Piles of money. But let me offer some perspective: the work I have described would cost "only" a fraction of the cost of a single one of the ten aircraft carriers the United States currently has planned and begun delivering as well as a fraction of what tens of countries each spend yearly on aid. Is this idea guaranteed to work in its entirety? Hardly. But I suspect that we, as a species, cannot afford to not try. The money absolutely exists. Does the will?

The natural dissemination of development is perhaps the ultimate measure of complete success. Everyone will benefit from organic growth, growth that is not created artificially. With the power of micro-loans, several thousand new companies will form. Gas stations will start popping up along the new roads and bus routes in Bangui. And nearby countries will want to connect to roads and rail for access to the CAR. They will want to connect to the energy infrastructure as well. And when people start getting energy, things tend to happen quickly. A lot of Central Africans will move home and bring with them an entrepreneurial drive. Hundreds of new types of companies are needed now – and those with some experience will flock to the CAR to satisfy this new demand. Be it printers, travel agents, or large-scale agricultural farmers, they will begin appearing where they are needed. There will also be several huge companies – notably energy and rail and telecommunications – that eventually will be state-controlled and that employ hundreds of thousands of people and turn over hundreds of millions of dollars annually.

What this project would accomplish is this: a whole country, a whole region, is given hope, is given a chance. The affluent parts of the world, by doing this, can show that needless suffering must and can end worldwide. We know that we personally win by helping others. We have shown that with some help, a country can prosper, and have happy and productive citizens. All lives matter. The whole world should have hope. And with some effort, it can.